My Self-Compassion Journal
cultivating Love & kindness for Myself

Written by Renee Jain

Illustrated by Nikki Abramowitz

brought to you by **www.zenThoughts.com**

"Self-compassion is approaching ourselves, our inner experience
with spaciousness, with the quality of allowing which has
a quality of gentleness. Instead of our usual tendency to want
to get over something, to fix it, to make it go away, the path
of compassion is totally different. Compassion allows."
- Robert Gonzales

After we face challenges and experience emotional turmoil, it's commonplace
to be self-critical. In short, we are regularly beating ourselves up for own
humanity. It's time to acknowledge that there are more options for how we
can react to adversity.

During the trials of life, we deserve our own love and kindness. This is not
about self-pity or self-indulgence, but rather, it's a form of compassion that
acknowledges we are simply human. Mounting research reveals that allowing
ourselves to "be human" is a path to greater well-being; but even without the
science, if we quiet our souls and listen to our inner voices, it is clear that
self-compassion will always trump self-criticism on the journey toward living
a purposeful, meaningful, and engaged life.

Use this journal, containing six research-inspired exercises, to nurture
greater self-compassion.

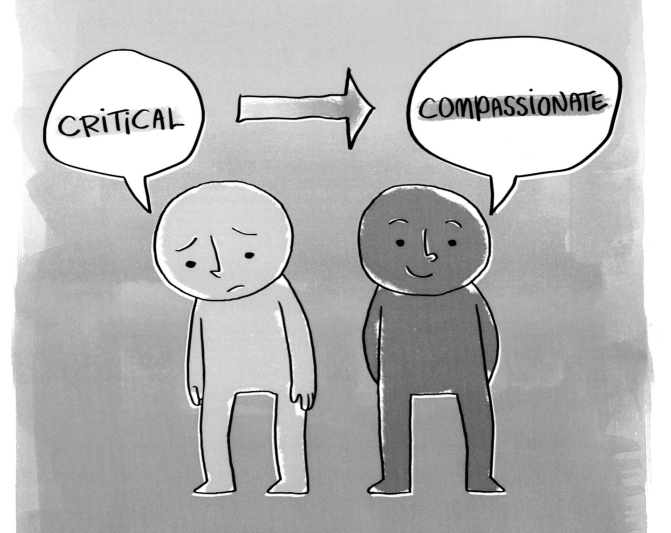

dear me, I choose
a new inner voice...

When your best friend comes to you
for advice, it's usually pretty easy
to be caring and compassionate.
What about when you have a problem--
how do you speak to yourself?

Think of a challenge
you're dealing with right now.

Take a deep breath and
write a letter to yourself in the
voice of your very best friend.

"A moment of self-compassion can change your entire day.
A string of such moments can change the course of your life."
- Christopher K. Germer

Dear me,

Love, me

Dear me,

Love, me

Dear me,

Love, me

Dear me,

Love, me

Dear me,

Love, me

Dear me,

Love, me

Dear me, I am
grateful for...

What do you love? Is it a hot cup of tea in the morning or a cold cup of milk? Is it being close to nature? Focus on the good stuff in your life--big or small.

Next, focus on one of these things, close your eyes, take a deep breath, and savor it.

Write about what you are grateful for in your life and how it makes you feel.

"Change the way you look at things and the things you look at change."
- Wayne W. Dyer

I'm grateful for...

I'm grateful for this that happened in the last 24 hours...

I'm grateful for this that happened in the last week...

This is how I feel when I think of these things or experiences...

I'm grateful for...

I'm grateful for...

I'm grateful for this that happened in the last 24 hours...

I'm grateful for this that happened in the last week...

This is how I feel when I think of these things or experiences...

I'm grateful for...

I'm grateful for...

I'm grateful for this that happened in the last 24 hours...

I'm grateful for this that happened in the last week...

This is how I feel when I think of these things or experiences...

I'm grateful for...

Dear me, this too shall pass...

Without minimizing any emotions or situations you currently face, please remember that this challenge will indeed pass. Allow yourself to go through the experience while still envisioning your better, brighter future ahead.

Imagine the best version of yourself 10 years down the line. What does that look like? What are you doing when you wake up in the morning?

What feelings do you have? What brings you fulfillment? Write about your best possible future self.

"You are the sky. Everything else--it's just the weather."
- Pema Chödrön

Dear me,

Love, me

Dear me,

Love, me

Dear me,

Love, me

Dear me,

Love, me

Dear me,

Love, me

Dear me,

Love, me

Dear me, this is
how I find my zen...

What relaxes you?
What puts your soul at ease?
When are you most calm, and
what triggers feeling of peace
when you are calm and relaxed?

Take a moment to write a
list of the people, places, and
things that bring you zen.

"What we achieve inwardly will change outer reality."
- Plutarch

HOW I find my zen:

1.

2.

3.

4.

5.

6.

7.

8.

9.

10.

HOW I find my Zen:

1.

2.

3.

4.

5.

6.

7.

8.

9.

10.

How I find my zen:

1.

2.

3.

4.

5.

6.

7.

8.

9.

10.

How I find my zen:

1.

2.

3.

4.

5.

6.

7.

8.

9.

10.

How I find my zen:

1.

2.

3.

4.

5.

6.

7.

8.

9.

10.

HOW I find my zen:

1.

2.

3.

4.

5.

6.

7.

8.

9.

10.

Dear me,
I'm here for you...

Some challenges are unavoidable,
but our reaction to these challenges
is almost always a choice.

If you're going through a tough time,
choose to treat yourself with
kindness, care, and compassion.

Remember, you are not alone.
Write a letter to yourself with a
reminder that it's okay to be human
and to feel different emotions.

*"Have patience with everything that remains
unsolved in your heart... Live in the question."
- Rainer Maria Rilke*

Dear me,

Love, me

Dear me,

Love, me

Dear me,

Love, me

Dear me,

Love, me

Dear me,

Love, me

Dear me,

Love, me

Dear me, these are
my superpowers...

Everyone has strengths or superpowers. Some people are funny; some are creative; others are determined.

What are your superpowers?
How have you used one recently?

How can your superpowers
help you solve a problem?

"Happiness can be found even in the darkest of times, when one only remembers to turn on the light."
- Albus Dumbledore

My superpowers are... (circle them!)

creativity   forgiveness   love

self-regulation   leadership

fairness   humility   kindness

perspective   honesty   zest

bravery   judgment   prudence

appreciation of beauty

perseverance   humor

curiosity   social intelligence

spirituality   hope   teamwork

love of learning   gratitude

More:

This is how I used one of my superpowers recently...

This is how one of my superpowers can help me solve a challenge I'm facing...

My superpowers are... (circle them!)

creativity   forgiveness   love

self-regulation   leadership

fairness   humility   kindness

perspective   honesty   zest

bravery   judgment   prudence

appreciation of beauty

perseverance   humor

curiosity   social intelligence

spirituality   hope   teamwork

love of learning   gratitude

More:

This is how I used one of my superpowers recently...

This is how one of my superpowers can help me solve a challenge I'm facing...

My superpowers are... (circle them!)

creativity forgiveness love

self-regulation leadership

fairness humility kindness

perspective honesty zest

bravery judgment prudence

appreciation of beauty

perseverance humor

curiosity social intelligence

spirituality hope teamwork

love of learning gratitude

More:

This is how I used one of my superpowers recently...

This is how one of my superpowers can help me solve a challenge I'm facing...

The Science

All of the exercises in this journal are inspired by research. While what you see below is not an exhaustive list, they are certainly great references for those looking to learn more about the science of self-compassion, resilience, and well-being.

Dear me, I choose a new inner voice...

Neff, K. (2011). *Self-compassion: Stop beating yourself up and leave insecurity behind.* New York: William Morrow.

Shapira, L. B., & Mongrain, M. (2010). "The benefits of self-compassion and optimism exercises for individuals vulnerable to depression." *Journal of Positive Psychology,* 5(5), 377-389.

Dear me, I am grateful for...

Emmons, R. A., & Mishra, A. (2012). "Why gratitude enhances well-being: What we know, what we need to know." In Sheldon, K., Kashdan, T., & Steger, M.F. (Eds.) *Designing the future of positive psychology: Taking stock and moving forward.* New York: Oxford University Press.

Dear me, this too shall pass...

King, A. (2001). "The health benefits of writing about life goals." *Personality and Social Psychology Bulletin,* 27(7), 798-807.

Seligman, M. (2006). *Learned optimism: How to change your mind and your life.* New York: Vintage Books.

Dear me, this is how I find my zen...

Williams, M., & Penman, D. (2011). *Mindfulness: An eight-week plan for finding peace in a frantic world.* Emmaus, Pa.: Rodale Books.

Dear me, I'm here for you...

Reivich, K. (2002). *The resilience factor: 7 essential skills for overcoming life's inevitable obstacles.* New York: Broadway Books.

Dear me, these are my superpowers...

Peterson, C., & Seligman, M. (2004). *Character strengths and virtues a handbook and classification.* Washington, DC: American Psychological Association.

Practice more self-compassion exercises at

www.ZenThoughts.com

20447964R10032

Made in the USA
Middletown, DE
26 May 2015